FREAKY
PHENOMENA

PERSONALITY

The Series

CONSCIOUSNESS
FAITH
HEALING
LIFE AFTER DEATH
MYSTERIOUS PLACES
PERSONALITY
PSYCHIC ABILITIES
THE SENSES

PERSONALITY

Don Rauf

Foreword by Joe Nickell, Senior Research Fellow, Committee for Skeptical Inquiry

MASON CREST

Mason Crest
450 Parkway Drive, Suite D Broomall, PA 19008
www.masoncrest.com

Printed in the United States of America

First printing
9 8 7 6 5 4 3 2 1

Series ISBN: 978-1-4222-3772-4
Hardcover ISBN: 978-1-4222-3778-6
ebook ISBN: 978-1-4222-8012-6

Cataloging-in-Publication Data is available on file at the Library of Congress.

Developed and Produced by Print Matters Productions, Inc. (www.printmattersinc.com)
Cover and Interior Design by: Bill Madrid, Madrid Design
Composition by Carling Design

Picture credits: 9, Morphart Creation/Shutterstock; 10, sdominick/iStock; 12, ambrozinio/Shutterstock; 12, Dmytro Zinkevych/Shutterstock; 14, JewelStudio/Shutterstock; 16, Wikimedia Commons; 17, Mary A Lupo/Shutterstock; 18, pathdoc/Shutterstock; 20, Rocketclips, Inc./Shutterstock; 21, pathdoc/Shutterstock; 23, Sergey Nivens/Shutterstock; 24, Dark Moon Pictures/Shutterstock; 26, mariapazmorales/iStock; 27, wenht/iStock; 29, Subbotina Anna/Shutterstock; 30, janulla/iStock; 34, KireevI/Shutterstock; 35, Ondine32/iStock; 36, GeorgeRudy/iStock; 38, karenfoleyphotography/iStock; 42, Maartje van Caspel/iStock

Cover: SKapl/iStoc

CONTENTS

KEY ICONS TO LOOK FOR:

Words to understand: These words with their easy-to-understand definitions will increase the reader's understanding of the text while building vocabulary skills.

Sidebars: This boxed material within the main text allows readers to build knowledge, gain insights, explore possibilities, and broaden their perspectives by weaving together additional information to provide realistic and holistic perspectives.

Educational Videos: Readers can view videos by scanning our QR codes, providing them with additional educational content to supplement the text. Examples include news coverage, moments in history, speeches, iconic sports moments and much more!

Series glossary of key terms: This back-of-the book glossary contains terminology used throughout this series. Words found here increase the reader's ability to read and comprehend higher-level books and articles in this field.

Advice From a Full-Time Professional Investigator of Strange Mysteries

I wish I'd had books like this when I was young. Like other boys and girls, I was intrigued by ghosts, monsters, and other freaky things. I grew up to become a stage magician and private detective, as well as (among other things) a literary and folklore scholar and a forensic-science writer. By 1995, I was using my varied background as the world's only full-time professional investigator of strange mysteries.

As I travel around the world, lured by its enigmas, I avoid both uncritical belief and outright dismissal. I insist mysteries should be *investigated* with the intent of solving them. That requires *critical thinking*, which begins by asking useful questions. I share three such questions here, applied to brief cases from my own files:

Is a particular story really true?

Consider Louisiana's Myrtles Plantation, supposedly haunted by the ghost of a murderous slave, Chloe. We are told that, as revenge against a cruel master, she poisoned three members of his family. Phenomena that ghost hunters attributed to her spirit included a mysteriously swinging door and unexplained banging noises.

The Discovery TV Channel arranged for me to spend a night there alone. I learned from the local historical society that Chloe never existed and her three alleged victims actually died in a yellow fever epidemic. I prowled the house, discovering that the spooky door was simply hung off center, and that banging noises were easily explained by a loose shutter.

Does a claim involve unnecessary assumptions?

In Flatwoods, WV, in 1952, some boys saw a fiery UFO streak across the evening sky and apparently land on a hill. They went looking for it, joined by others. A flashlight soon revealed a tall creature with shining eyes and a face shaped like the ace of spades. Suddenly, it swooped at them with "terrible claws," making a high-pitched hissing sound. The witnesses fled for their lives.

Half a century later, I talked with elderly residents, examined old newspaper accounts, and did other research. I learned the UFO had been a meteor. Descriptions of the creature almost perfectly matched a barn owl—seemingly tall because it had perched on a tree limb. In contrast, numerous incredible assumptions would be required to argue for a flying saucer and an alien being.

Is the proof as great as the claim?

A Canadian woman sometimes exhibited the crucifixion wounds of Jesus—allegedly produced supernaturally. In 2002, I watched blood stream from her hands and feet and from tiny scalp wounds like those from a crown of thorns.

However, because her wounds were already bleeding, they could have been self-inflicted. The lance wound that pierced Jesus' side was absent, and the supposed nail wounds did not pass through the hands and feet, being only on one side of each. Getting a closer look, I saw that one hand wound was only a small slit, not a large puncture wound. Therefore, this extraordinary claim lacked the extraordinary proof required.

These three questions should prove helpful in approaching claims and tales in Freaky Phenomena. I view the progress of science as a continuing series of solved mysteries. Perhaps you too might consider a career as a science detective. You can get started right here.

Joe Nickell
Senior Research Fellow, Committee for Skeptical Inquiry
Amherst, NY

STRANGE BRAINS

O f all the unexplained locations in the universe, the most mysterious place of all may be one that's very near to you: the human brain. The organ inside the cranium can take people down some twisty passageways where they end up acting in puzzling ways.

One very mystifying neurological disorder makes people see objects as much, much smaller than they are in real life. People with Alice in Wonderland syndrome, as it's called, live life as if they're looking through the wrong end of a microscope. They have *micropsia*, which causes things to appear small, and sometimes they might have *macropsia*, which makes items appear big. In the *New York Times* in 2014, a woman with the syndrome wrote how furniture a few feet away often looked as if it could fit in a dollhouse. The ailment is most likely brought on by a change in the brain—possibly linked to migraines, stress, schizophrenia, psychoactive drugs, brain tumors, or infections. Most cases have been reported in children between 5 and 10 years old.

If you've ever had the urge to eat yourself up, you might have *autosarcophagy*. It can result from Lesch-Nyan syndrome, a condition that spurs people to mutilate themselves. Young children mostly get the disease. They cannot control their muscles, and they develop an irresistible urge to be self-destructive, often chewing fingertips and lips.

Imagine if your hand had a mind of its own and did things without you wanting it to, such as pinching someone, touching a stranger's face, tearing off clothes, or even strangling yourself. That's exactly what can happen if you have alien hand syndrome, or anarchic hand, as it's sometimes called. With this neurological disorder, a person's hand functions involuntarily. In rare cases, the hand might try to force-feed the individual. New Jersey resident Karen Byrne, who has such a rogue limb, described the difficulties on CBS News in 2013. She said, "I would make a telephone call

and this hand would hang up the phone
… I would light a cigarette and this one
would put it out. I would be drinking cof-
fee and this hand would dump it." This
ailment is different from typical involuntary limb movement in that the hand is
goal oriented—its motion has a purpose.
It can occur after brain surgery, stroke,
infection, tumor, aneurysm, or specific
degenerative brain conditions such as
Alzheimer's disease and Creutzfeldt-Ja-
kob disease.

When it comes to freaky phenomena, these disorders of the mind are
very unusual. This volume takes a more
in-depth look at a few prominent mental infirmities—multiple personality disorder, foreign accent syndrome, Cotard
delusion (the delusion of being dead),
Capgras syndrome (face blindness), and
Munchausen syndrome.

At one point in Lewis Carroll's Alice's
Adventures in Wonderland *Alice doubles
in size and sees objects much, much, smaller
than they are in real life. The neurological
disorder, micropsia, causes things to appear
small, similar to Alice's experience.*

CHAPTER 1

MULTIPLE PERSONALITY DISORDER

Dissociative identity disorder is a mental health problem that affects about 2 percent of the population.

Having "multiple personalities" is a mental health problem that is often associated with villains in the movies and on TV. In 2017, the director M. Night Shyamalan, who is known for his twist endings, released the film *Split*. The picture stars James MacAvoy as a murderer with two dozen personalities who kidnaps three girls. The hostages must negotiate and interact with each one to try and escape the deadliest identity within their captor's mind.

The fact is, most people with this **chronic** emotional illness are not murderous at all, and many in the medical field criticize such a depiction because it paints these patients in a negative light. Research has shown that they are far more likely to hurt themselves than other people.

Today, the condition is called **dissociative** identity disorder (DID) and the National Alliance on Mental Illness (NAMI) says that about 2% of the population experience dissociative disorders.

In a 2016 article in the *Charlotte Observer,* reporter Amanda Harris described the interesting case of Amelia Joubert, an 18-year-old high school student who in many ways acted like a typical teen. Like most other DID patients, Joubert was a functional, responsible person. Many with the condition hold steady jobs, complete college degrees, and succeed as spouses and parents.

One part of her life wasn't normal, however—she was often troubled by voices she heard in her head. At first, Joubert thought the voices were coming from ghosts. In the article, she says, "For the longest time, I had no idea what was going on with me."

The voices then grew in strength until they were taking control of her mind, which NAMI says is typ-

Words to Understand

Chronic: Persisting for a long time or constantly recurring (used to describe illness).

Dissociative: Characterized by disconnection or separation.

Trauma: A deeply distressing or disturbing experience.

Childhood trauma can often be directly linked with DID.

ical of the disease. The voices take on distinct personalities called *alters*. In Joubert's case, she would sometimes talk in different voices. She would adopt a Southern accent and become a four-year-old who loved kittens and horses. Or she'd turn into a five-year-old who wanted everyone to be happy. Sometimes, an older teen would appear to take care of the younger ones, or in a social situation, the voice of an extroverted personality would step forward.

When she went to psychotherapy to address her continuing problem, Joubert was diagnosed with DID. Conversations with medical professionals revealed that she had experienced childhood **trauma**, which most likely led her to develop 12 main alternate personalities inside her mind. She thinks of these distinct characters as individuals who contribute to her whole being.

Meet a mother with 20 personalities.

Therapy can be extremely helpful for those suffering with mental disorders.

When one of her alters takes over, she later has no recollection of what happened during that time. Through therapy, she has learned to communicate with these other identities to learn what happened when a period of her life seems to have been erased. By embracing the voices within, Joubert has learned to function better and move forward in her everyday life.

Scientific Take: Dividing and Conquering the Problems Within

Dissociative disorders are survivor mechanisms that most often form in children who have been exposed to long-term physical, sexual, or emotional abuse. Natural disasters and combat can also cause dissociative disorders. In some cases in which a young person is in a desperate situation with no hope for a relief, the mind reconfigures itself into different personalities to deal with the stressful situation or dissociates from reality in order to cope. Often these identities

Related Conditions

Losing Yourself: Dissociative Amnesia
With this condition, a person forgets major life details. Like DID, it is also triggered by traumatic events. At age 32, Naomi Lewis of England woke up one day in 2009 believing she was 15 again. All memory of the 17 years in between had evaporated. Doctors determined that severe stress had led to a dramatic memory loss. She couldn't even remember her 10-year-old son.

Unplugged from Reality: Depersonalization Disorder
With a continuing sense of being disconnected from reality, people with this disorder feel unplugged from normal thoughts, emotions, and actions. Rather than feeling engaged like an average person, they feel like they are watching a movie. Adam Duritz, singer in the group The Counting Crows, has grappled with this type of condition. In an interview in *Men's Health* in 2008, he said, "I have a form of dissociative disorder that makes the world seem like it's not real, as if things aren't taking place. It's hard to explain, but you feel untethered."

may have unique names, characteristics, mannerisms, and voices. Women are more likely to experience dissociative identity disorder than men. Various medications and therapies can help patients live with the disorder. To help patients move forward, a therapist may deal directly with each individual personality, helping that identity come to terms with what happened in the past.

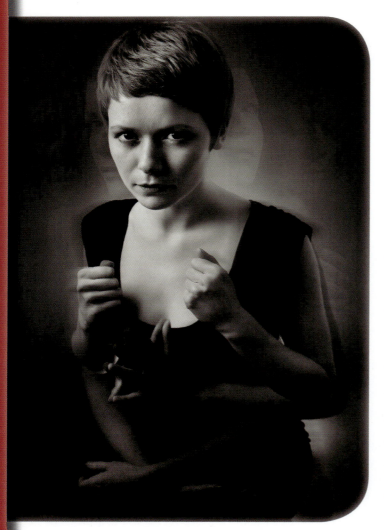

At times, severe stress can lead to mental deterioration.

The Woman with 100 Personalities

Kim Noble of South London may hold the not-so-welcome title of having the most multiple personalities ever. Mental health specialists discovered that she has more than 100 personalities, of all different ages, some female and some male, jockeying for position in her mind. As reported in the *Guardian* in 2011, Noble says she goes through about three or four switches a day from one personality to another. There is 15-year-old Judy who is bulimic, thinks she is fat, and appears only at mealtimes. Ken wears his hair up and keeps his shoulders back in a cocky stance. Spirit of Water is an entity that arrives only at bath time. In her autobiography, *All of Me*, Noble reveals several traumas that led to her split personality, including repeated abuse as a child and an arson attack. Ongoing therapy helps Noble live with her very crowded inner life. A psychotherapist who treated Noble says her DID is a remarkable coping device. Noble says that one of the most difficult parts is not remembering what happened when a personality takes over. When she returns to her prime self, keys are lost, pizzas arrive mysteriously, and the car may turn up parked miles from home.

A Case of Mistaken Identity?

DID was a key component in a case of assault. In 1990, Mark Peterson met a young woman in a bar in Oshkosh, WI, where they supposedly hit it off. When the two left, he asked if they could be more intimate in his car. Although the woman agreed, a few days later, Peterson was arrested for assault. The woman, who had 21 different personalities, said that Peterson took advantage of one of her weaker identities, coaxing the naive and compliant one to have sex, while her other personalities certainly did not want to be so intimate. He was initially found guilty of taking advantage of someone who was mentally ill, although his conviction was overturned a short time later. Reportedly, the woman's personality count increased to 46 during the time between the incident and the trial.

My Bad Side Did It

Multiple personality disorder has been used as a defense in a few crime cases. In October of 1977, Billy Milligan was arrested for attacking three women on the Ohio State University campus in Columbus. One of his victims said he was very nice but acted like a three-year-old girl. Another said he spoke in a German accent. After he was arrested, psychologist Dorothy Turner of Southwest Community Mental Health Center diagnosed him as having multiple personality disorder. Doctors observed at least 24 different identities and labeled 14 as "undesirables." These characters included Arthur, a proper Englishman; a Yugoslavian man named Ragen; the manipulative Allen; the con artist Tommy; and even an affection-starved teenage lesbian named Adalana. Milligan became the first person in American history to be found not guilty due to DID.

Billy Mulligan was the first person in America to be found not guilty due to dissociative identity disorder.

After spending a decade in mental hospitals, he was released when it was thought his personalities had melded. As of 2015, Leonardo DiCaprio was slated to star in a movie version of Milligan's life to be titled *The Crowded Room.*

In Fort Myers, FL, in 1981, Juanita Maxwell, a hotel chambermaid, was absolved of murder because of dissociative identity disorder. The 23-year-old beat, bit, and choked a 73-year-old guest to death. When she was arrested with blood on her shoes and a scratch on her face, she was surprised, telling officers she had no memory of the crime. A psychiatrist who visited her as she stood trial determined that Maxwell coped with multiple personalities. Ordinarily, Maxwell was a quiet, soft-spoken woman who seemed unlikely to commit such a violent act. But in conversations with the mental health worker, Juanita would disappear and another person would come to the forefront. This woman was a laughing and rowdy "Wanda Weston," who remembered the horrific crime in detail. Wanda told how she beat the woman to death with a lamp because of an argument about a pen. Ultimately, a judge ruled that Maxwell was not guilty by reason of insanity and committed her to a mental hospital. When Maxwell heard the verdict, she hugged her husband and in tears, she repeatedly told him, "I love you!" The sight was odd to some because only a short time before, while on the stand as "Wanda," she told the court how she had planned to murder her husband.

Football star Herschel Walker who wrote a book about his experience with dissociative identity disorder.

A Sports Star Tackles DID

In his book *Breaking Free: My Life with Dissociative Identity Disorder,* football star and 1982 Heisman Trophy winner Herschel Walker talked about acquiring multiple personalities after his life went off the tracks when his sports career ended. Some of his alters were the Hero, the Coach, the Enforcer, the Consoler, the Warrior, and the Daredevil. After 10 years of therapy, Walker pulled his life—and personalities— back together and got on a more stable path.

CHAPTER 2

FOREIGN ACCENT SYNDROME

Foreign accent syndrome is
frustrating for those who have it.

Lisa Alamia, a young mother and native of Rosenberg, TX, had never seen *Downton Abbey* or any other British shows. She had never visited England. She always spoke with a Southern twang. But after she underwent surgery on her jaw to correct an overbite in 2016, her speech dramatically changed. Instead of talking in her Texan drawl, she woke up sounding like someone from Southern England, or maybe someone who had lived awhile in Australia.

"I was very shocked," Alamia told *ABC News*. "I didn't know how to take it. I was very confused. I said 'y'all' all the time before the accent. Once I got the accent, I started noticing I'd say, 'You all.'"

Then she came home to her children. They were baffled. They thought she was playing some sort of joke. Because she was afraid other people would think the same, she stayed quiet for a long time. She found it hard to stay connected to her Hispanic heritage too—she couldn't even pronounce the word *tamales* the way she once did.

Alamia may find she's talking this way for a long time—the condition, known as foreign accent syndrome can be permanent. Usually caused by a brain injury, the syndrome is very rare. Only about 100 people have had it in the last century. Cases have included accent changes from Japanese to Korean, British English to French, American to British English, and Spanish to Hungarian.

Words to Understand

Affliction: Something that causes pain or suffering.

Multiple sclerosis: A chronic, typically progressive disease involving damage to the sheaths of nerve cells in the brain and spinal cord.

Psychological: Related to the mental and emotional state of a person.

Stroke: When blood flow to an area in the brain is cut off, depriving the brain of oxygen and glucose needed to survive.

Brain damage can trigger certain speech disorders like foreign accent syndrome.

Scientific Take: A Sudden Shift in the Brain

In most cases, some type of brain damage triggers foreign accent syndrome, sometimes referred to as the speech disorder *dysprosody*. The cause may be traumatic brain injury, a small **stroke**, or even **multiple sclerosis** or conversion disorder (a condition in which a person shows **psychological** stress in physical ways). The shock to the system and damage to the speech area of the brain alter speech in terms of timing, rhythm, intensity, intonation, and tongue position so that speech sounds foreign. The speech itself doesn't sound garbled; it remains highly intelligible. Certain blood vessels in the brain can be prone to blockages and they may affect articulation and comprehension. When they are damaged from a stroke, head injury, or possible surgery or other trauma,

A woman wakes from surgery with a British accent.

language patterns may shift. Toronto-based speech-language pathologist Regina Jokel says that the altered speech doesn't mean the person has an actual foreign accent but simply a speech impairment that makes him or her sound foreign.

A New Dialect from the Dentist

When Karen Butler of Toledo, OR, paid a visit to the dentist to have a few teeth removed in 2009, she didn't expect to have her native accent yanked along with them. After she woke up with her mouth sore and swollen postsurgery, she talked oddly. The dentist told her that her voice would return to normal once the swelling went down. Although she had never traveled to Europe or lived in a foreign country, her speech following the procedure sounded as if she were a mix of English, Irish, and a little Transylvanian. She pronounced *W*s like *V*s, as in "I *vant* to suck your blood." Other than the teasing she received from friends and family, Butler has suffered no other ill health or side effects. Although some people become depressed, isolated,

How a person speaks is part of their identity. Suddenly speaking in an accent not your own can be very disturbing.

and self-conscious with the **affliction**, Butler takes a light-hearted view and has found that she is more outgoing—she always has something to talk about.

One of the most notorious cases of foreign accent syndrome occurred during World War II in Norway. Germans occupied the country from 1940 to 1945, and during an air raid in 1941, shrapnel hit a Norwegian local named Astrid L. The 30-year-old's skull splintered, leaving her brain partially exposed. When she recovered, her health was totally normal except for one thing: She sounded as if she were speaking in a German or possibly French accent. Having a German accent was far from popular with the despised German enemy occupying the country. As a result of her new accent, Astrid's countrymen often turned their backs on her and refused to

Even More Strange: A Total Lingual Shift

Perhaps even more puzzling but related to foreign accent syndrome are the few cases in which a person suddenly finds him- or herself speaking an entirely different language. When Dujomir Marasovic, a 13-year-old Croatian girl, awoke from a 24-hour coma in 2010, she was only able to communicate in German. Her family needed a translator to speak with her. In another case from 2007, a crash knocked out a Czech race-car driver, Matej Kus. When medics revived him, he could speak perfect English in a clear British accent. His newfound language skills quickly faded however. He hopes to still regain fluency in English but wants to learn "without someone having to hit me over the head first."

Australian Ben McMahon studied a minimal amount of Mandarin Chinese in high school, but after whacking his head in a car accident, he was suddenly fluent. On the one hand, he was so good that he got a job giving tours of Melbourne to Chinese tourists. But on the other hand, he had to put in some time to relearn English. When 25-year-old Roy Curtis of Birmingham, England, flipped his van, bashing his head and pelvis in the crash, he went into a coma. Upon waking, he not only spoke fluent French, he felt certain that he was actually the actor Matthew McConaughey. His new talent and new-found celebrity lifestyle faded in two months as he made a full recovery.

Scientists have speculated that such a complete language eruption may occur because damage to part of the brain that controls the muscles used to produce speech perhaps trigger some hidden talent with languages. But speaking a whole other language is much more elaborate than talking in an accent, and so far doctors have been unable to explain with certainty how it occurs.

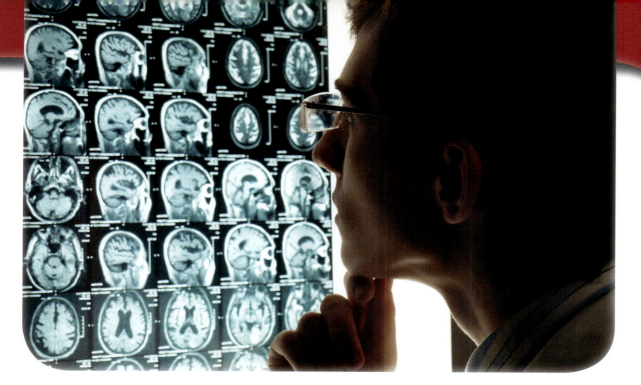

Although there is some speculation, doctors aren't sure how total lingual shifts and foreign accents can be reversed.

serve her in shops. She remained isolated and stigmatized until the end of the war. Astrid's story became one of the best know historical accounts of foreign language syndrome because her neurologist, George Herman Monrad-Krohn, wrote a detailed account of her disorder.

Car Crash to a Tongue Twister

When Leanne Rowe of Tasmania was in a car crash in 2005, doctors treated her for head trauma, a broken back, and an injured jaw. As her jaw healed, she began to communicate but with slurred words—a side effect from her medication, according to medical attendants. Gradually, the slur evolved into a French accent—a far cry from her native Aussie tongue. In an interview with *ABC News*, Rowe said that the condition made her angry because she was Australian and wanted to sound like herself. The condition has led her to feel depressed, anxious, and reluctant to speak in public.

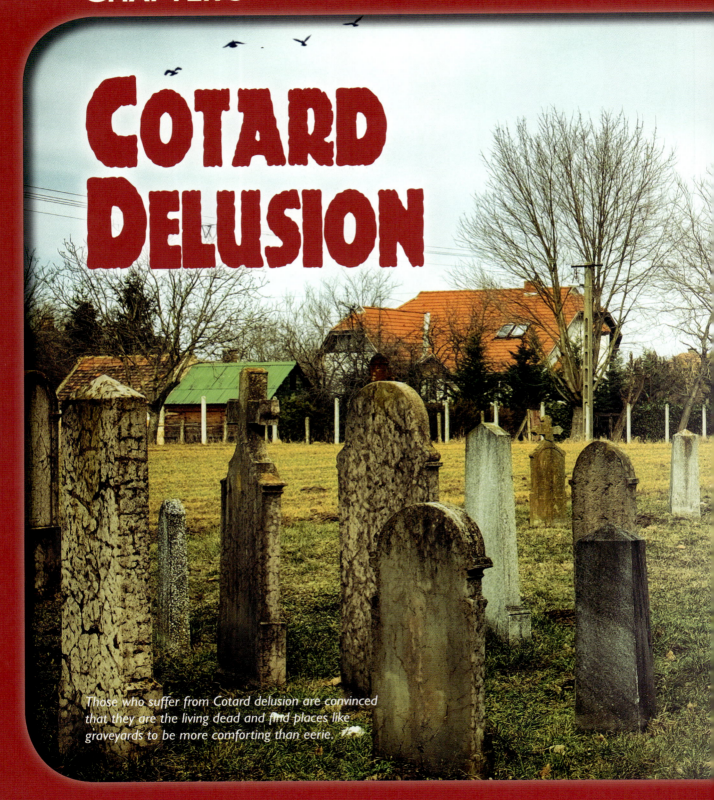

CHAPTER 3

COTARD DELUSION

Those who suffer from Cotard delusion are convinced that they are the living dead and find places like graveyards to be more comforting than eerie.

With pop culture's zombie fixation stronger than ever (as seen in television shows like *The Walking Dead* and movies such as *World War Z*), it's maybe surprising that more people aren't suffering from Cotard **delusion** (also known as "walking corpse syndrome"). Those afflicted with the ultra-rare disorder are much more than dead tired—they are convinced they are no longer living, although quite clearly they are alive.

Haley Smith of Alabama developed Cotard delusion a short time after her parents divorced. Struggling with her parents' separation, the 14-year-old was sitting in class one day, when she had a strange sensation that she was no longer breathing. The feeling did not go away. As it persisted, Smith felt compelled to visit graveyards, seeking comfort in those who were already dead.

She missed days at school, sleeping at home and staying awake through the night. In an interview in 2015 with the *Daily Mail*, she said, "I'd fantasize about having picnics in graveyards and I'd spend a lot of time watching horror films because seeing the zombies made me feel relaxed, like I was with family."

Believing she was utterly dead, Smith decided to no longer worry about dieting. She began eating whatever and how much she wanted—after all, why not eat whatever you like if you're dead. Her

Words to Understand

Bipolar disease: A mental disorder characterized by alternating periods of elation and depression.

Delusion: A persistent false belief about the self or persons or objects outside the self.

Psychosis: A severe mental disorder in which thought and emotions are so impaired that the patient loses touch with external reality.

Putrefy: To decay and rot and produce an offensive smell.

Schizophrenia: A long-term mental disorder involving a breakdown in the relation between thought, emotion, and behavior.

physical and mental health deteriorated rapidly. After two years battling with this odd and all-consuming feeling, she opened up to her father, who was very understanding and arranged for her to see a psychiatrist. The doctor diagnosed her condition as Cotard delusion, a psychological disorder in which a person believes that he or she doesn't exist, or parts of the body don't exist. Analysis and talking sessions paved the way for Smith's recovery. She also said that Disney films (*The Little Mermaid, Aladdin, Sleeping Beauty,* and *Bambi*), along with a sympathetic and affectionate boyfriend, drew her out of her dark place after three years of living as a dead person.

Scientific Take: The Life of the Living Dead

Cotard delusion is a rare mental illness that causes the patient to hold an unshakeable, delusional belief that he or she is already dead, does not exist, and might be rotting away or **putrefying**. Some of the afflicted believe that parts of their body, blood, and/or organs are gone. Although most people with the disorder deny they even exist, about half of the patients who have the disease think they are immortal. Patients may have a belief that things around them are dead and that the world will soon be destroyed.

Like **bipolar disease** or **schizophrenia**, Cotard's is a type of delusional **psychosis**, and is linked to clinical depression. The disorder has been known to occur in people who also suffer from multiple sclerosis, migraines, and hypochondria. It is thought to result from misfiring of neurons in the fusiform gyrus, part of the brain that recognizes faces, and the amygdala, a section that

Just like an aging piece of fruit, those who suffer from Cotard delusion feel as though they are decaying.

processes emotions and links them to a recognized face. These two effects combined leave an individual with a distorted reality. In addition to talk therapy and analysis, treatment may include antidepressants, antipsychotics, and controversial electroconvulsive therapy. A positron emission tomography (PET) scan of one Cotard's patient revealed an almost vegetative state.

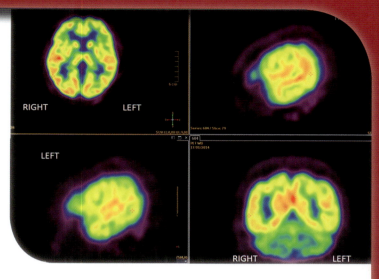

A PET scan of a human brain.

Brain Dead

In 2013, *New Scientist* interviewed a British man with Cotard's identified as "Graham." Graham had been suffering from severe depression and tried to kill himself by taking an electrical appliance with him into the bath. Eight months later, he told doctors that he had killed his brain. The physicians tried to reassure him that he couldn't be talking without a brain, but Graham didn't believe them. "I just got annoyed. I didn't know how I could speak or do anything with no brain, but as far as I was concerned I hadn't got one," he recalled in the interview.

A Discovery in Paris

Dr. Jules Cotard was a Parisian neurologist who in 1880 first described what he called the *délire des negations* (delirium of negations), now known as Cotard's syndrome or Cotard delusion. Cotard discovered the disorder in a woman who had depression along with symptoms of psychosis. Although Mademoiselle X believed she didn't have a brain or intestines and didn't need to eat, she thought she would live forever. Despite believing that she was immortal, she died of starvation. Cotard's detailed study of the condition gained widespread acceptance and the disease was eventually named after him.

Graham lost all interest in things and people. When doctors scanned his brain, they observed that his mind was functioning like someone who was under anesthesia or was asleep although he was fully awake. Graham lost his sense of smell and taste, and stopped brushing his teeth, which eventually turned black. He would make occasional visits to the graveyard. Through psycho-therapy and medication, Graham slowly came out of his catatonic state and regained his ability to take pleasure in life although he said in *New Scientist*, "Things just feel a bit bizarre sometimes."

Learn more about Cotard syndrome.

The Deceased and the Reeking

In New York in 2003, when a "Ms. Lee" told her family that she was dead and reeked of rotting flesh, she demanded to be taken to the morgue. After being admitted to a psychiatric ward, Ms. Lee was diagnosed with Cotard delusion, received antipsychotic drugs, and after about a month she regained her mental health and was released.

Belgian psychiatrists wrote of treating a 46-year-old woman who said she hadn't slept in a year or eaten or gone to the bathroom in months. She claimed her organs had decayed, her heart had no beat, and all her blood was gone. Therapy and medication over the course of 10 months brought her back to a functional state.

Other Delusional Disorders

Just as some people think they are zombies, others believe they are werewolves or vampires.

Clinical Lycanthropy

People with this mental disorder hold that they are a wolf or some other type of animal. The condition may have roots in a superstition that people can change into werewolves. The disor-der is extremely rare—about 56 cases have been recorded since 1850, according to research by Dr. Jan Dirk Blom, an assistant professor of psychiatry at the University of Groningen, the Netherlands, published in 2014 in the journal *History of Psychiatry*. That study also noted cases in which individuals were convinced they were a dog, a snake, a frog, or a bee.

The November 1975 issue of *The Canadian Psychiatric Association Journal* reported on several cases of lycanthropy, including that of a 37-year-old man, who was admitted to the hospital after repeated public displays of bizarre activity, including howling at the moon, sleeping in cemeteries, allowing his hair and beard to grow out, and lying in the center of busy highways. He was diagnosed as psychotic and successfully treated with antipsychotic medication.

Clinical Vampirism

Psychiatrists have long been aware of cases in which someone lives with a delusional notion that he or she is a vampire and must consume human blood. Also called Renfield's syndrome after a character in Bram Stoker's novel *Dracula*, clinical vampirism was the diagnosis for Richard Trenton Chase who in 1979 committed a spree of six sordid murders in Sacramento, CA. He drank his victims' blood and cannibalized their remains. When finally locked behind bars, he continued to ask for blood, until he finally killed himself.

Most with the condition are male and often have schizophrenia. *Autovampirism* is a variation of the disease where the afflicted have an urge to drink their own blood. Another syndrome, zoophagia, appears to be related as patients with this disorder may go on to develop clinical vampirism. People with zoophagia have an unnatural urge to consume living creatures such as cats, dogs, and birds.

There are people who are afflicted with the urge to drink human blood.

CHAPTER 4

CAPGRAS SYNDROME

The amygdala, an almond-shaped region of the
brain that processes emotions and memories,
is thought to be the source of Capgras syndrome.

In the movie *Invasion of the Body Snatchers*, aliens replace humans with identical copies cloned in pods. Those who have Capgras syndrome or delusion have an irrational belief that their friends, spouse, family members, or even pets have been substituted with imposters. A few patients become so **paranoid** that they think that they themselves have been replaced.

In 2011, the *Psychiatric Times* published an account of a 40-year-old mother who insisted that her 9-year-old daughter had been taken by child protective services and that the child living with her was not really her daughter. Sometimes, when the mother would show up at school to pick up her daughter, she would pull away from her child and scream, "Give me my real daughter; I know what you've done!" She told people of instances where she spotted her real daughter being driven in a car by a stranger, but the daughter was "whisked away before I could talk to her."

When friends and family finally got her to undergo a psychiatric evaluation, health care workers diagnosed her with Capgras syndrome. Doctors prescribed that the mother take risperidone, a drug commonly used to treat schizophrenia and bipolar disorder. After two months on the medication,

Words to Understand

Alzheimer's: Progressive mental deterioration that can occur in middle or old age, due to generalized degeneration of the brain.

Atrophy: To waste away, especially due to underuse or neglect.

Epilepsy: A neurological disorder marked by sudden recurrent episodes of sensory disturbance, loss of consciousness, or convulsions.

Narcoleptic: Related to a chronic sleep disorder. Narcoleptics suffer from chronic daytime sleepiness and can fall asleep unexpectedly.

Paranoid: Related to a mental condition involving intense anxious or fearful feelings and thoughts often related to persecution, threat, or conspiracy.

however, the mother still would not accept her daughter as her own. Eventually, social services had to step in and take custody of the girl. The daughter said, "I love my mother except for when she doesn't believe I'm me."

While treatment did not work in this case, therapy and antipsychotic medications can often help a Capgras patient return to normal.

Scientific Take: Who Are You? A Failure to Recognize

Opinions differ about the causes of Capgras syndrome. Many scientists believe that Capgras syndrome can be brought on by a simple failure of normal recognition processes following brain damage from a stroke, drug overdose, accident, or some other damage to the brain. Researchers have also reported that lesions on the brain, signs of cerebral **atrophy**, **epilepsy**, and **Alzheimer's** may be connected to the syndrome. Scientists suspect that the disorder is connected to a misfiring in the amygdala, which processes emotions and memories and gauges the emotional significance of what a person sees. One psychoanalytical theory holds that the disorder could be triggered by emotional trauma or repressed feeling—the brain is reacting to complex psychological issues, such as those dealing with troubled parental relationships.

Whatever the cause, Capgras patients have a breakdown between the part of the brain that processes visual information and the portion of the brain that handles emotional response. A few scientists attribute the disease to disruption in memory management—individuals with Capgras have severe problems with memory storage and retrieval. Because they process new information without tying it to prior memories, they can't connect the person in front of them to someone they already know. Blind people can also have Capgras delusion—they hear a voice of someone in their lives but do not trust that it is really that person.

A marker for the disease is galvanic skin response—the reaction of our skin sweating in correspondence to emotional excitement. When Capgras patients see familiar faces, they have no increase in galvanic response. Health care workers treat Capgras patients with therapy that helps overcome delusions, as well as medications that counteract psychosis and mood disorders. Talk therapy may include discussions about a patient's evidence for the belief and guiding the individual to the conclusion that the substitution is delusional based on available evidence.

A neuroscientist presents a case of Capgras syndrome.

Killing the Enemies

In 1989, the *Bulletin of the American Academy of Psychiatry* published an account of a 37-year-old man who was convinced that his father, sister, nephew, brother, and brother-in-law had all died and clones had replaced them. He also believed that former presidents and members of Congress were all imposters. The man had lost his brother to suicide.

According to the man, voices told him that a spirit who was controlling his father's body had killed his brother. The mentally ill man knew he had to destroy this spirit so he shot and murdered his father. The man went on to shoot his nephew and a stranger across the street whom he thought was an accomplice. He intended to hunt down and shoot his other imposter relatives as well but was captured before he could carry out his plan. The man was found not guilty by reason of insanity and placed on antipsychotic medications and therapy.

The Delusion of Look-alikes

French psychiatrist Jean Marie Joseph Capgras is credited with identifying this disorder in 1923, along with fellow investigator Jean Reboul-Lachaux. They studied the case of a French woman who swore that doubles had taken the place of her husband, friends, and acquaintances. She distanced herself from these people, thinking that a new double replaced the person each time he or she left the room. She was convinced that she had had at least 80 husbands. The researchers dubbed the ailment "*l'illusion des sosies*," which translates as "the illusion of look-alikes."

What Have You Done with My Husband?

In an interview on National Public Radio (NPR), Carol Berman, a psychiatrist at New York University Medical Center, told the story of a female patient who came to her office deeply concerned because she had found a man in her house recently who was calmly sitting on her couch, dressed in her husband's clothes. She felt strangely empty gazing at him. Who was this man? She was certain her real husband had been swapped out.

Oddly enough, Dr. Berman's own husband had begun suffering from Capgras syndrome as a result of dementia. She said that due to his brain deterioration, he thought an imposter was walking through the door instead of her. In the interview she said, "I hope he's recognizing me, but you never know what you're going to get when you get back home."

The Man in the Mirror

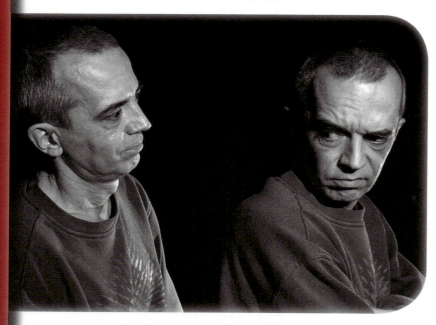

Not being able to recognize yourself in the mirror can be unsettling for those suffering with Capgras syndrome.

In 2015, the journal *Neurocase* described the case of a 78-year-old divorced man and father of four identified as Mr. B. Every day, Mr. B. would see a man in the mirror who looked like him, moved liked him, and dressed like him, but he was certain that this person was a fake. He recognized all his family members, it was only the man in the mirror who disturbed him.

After about a week and a half of being haunted by this stranger, Mr. B. said that the twin began acting hostile toward him. His physicians prescribed him an antidepressant and an antipsychotic that are both often used to treat Alzheimer's. After three months, his delusion ended. Mr. B. now sees himself in the mirror instead of a strange body double.

The Replacements

Dr. V. S. Ramachandran, director of the Center for Brain and Cognition at the University of California, San Diego, and Dr. Todd Feinberg, associate professor of neurology and psychiatry at the Albert Einstein College of Medicine in New York, noted these Capgras cases:

- A man who thought his poodle was replaced with an identical but different dog.
- A patient who swore his running shoes were substituted with identical fakes every morning.
- An individual who claimed that dishes and towels were replaced each day with exact replicas of the ones that had been there the night before.

Double Trouble: Syndrome of Subjective Doubles

With this disorder, which is very similar to Capgras delusion, a patient believes he or she has a double (or doppelgänger) with the same appearance, but usually with different character traits, who is leading a life of their own. The doppelgänger has been a popular theme in literature and film.

Although believing one has an identical physical double is a popular device in fiction, it's rare in real life.

CHAPTER 5

MUNCHAUSEN SYNDROME

Munchausen syndrome by proxy can be dangerous and sometimes fatal for children. When a parent falsely believes that their child is sick the situation can take a deadly turn.

People with the mental disorder Munchausen syndrome have a desperate need to be seen as ill when they are not really physically sick. Those afflicted either pretend to be sick or they take action to produce symptoms of illness. The syndrome is tied to severe emotional difficulties and those who suffer from it have an extreme need for attention—they are eager to visit the doctor or hospital and submit to a range of tests.

The condition is similar to **hypochondria**, which causes individuals to worry obsessively about being ill even though they have no apparent illness. The difference is hypochondriacs believe they are really sick, whereas people with Munchausen syndrome will consciously fake symptoms to get the attention they need to meet their severe emotional and self-esteem problems. The irony of the disease is that those who have it really are ill mentally, although they typically only admit to physical sickness.

The syndrome got its name from a literary character named Baron von Munchausen who appeared in a German book written in 1785. In the book, the character tells many wild, impossible, fantastic stories about himself. Like Baron Munchausen, those with the syndrome are known to exaggerate their condition or embellish stories about their life.

Sometimes it can be difficult to tell the difference between someone with Munchausen syndrome and a **charlatan**. In 2010, a woman in New York City pretended to have leukemia and raised

Words to Understand

Charlatan: A fraud.

Factitious: Artificially created or developed.

Hypochondria: Extreme depression centered on imaginary physical ailments.

Manipulating: Influencing the behavior or emotions of others for one's own purposes.

Narcissistic: Having an excessive interest in oneself.

Hypochondria forces people to believe that they are ill when really there is nothing wrong.

money for her treatment. The funds actually went to pay for her wedding, and she did not have cancer at all. That same year, a 28-year-old woman announced that she was the victim of a random acid attack, which disfigured her. After going on *Oprah*, she admitted that she had disfigured herself. True Munchausen's is not about financial gain but emotional satisfaction. Sometimes, however, the two overlap. The acid attack seemed to fit the definition because the woman was desperately seeking attention.

In 2010, *Time* magazine published an interview with Dr. Marc Feldman, a clinical professor of psychiatry at the University of Alabama. He said that the condition may be more common than one might think: "In hospital [studies], it's estimated that between 1% and 5% of patients have to some extent faked or exaggerated their illnesses. In psychiatric hospitals, it's a little higher: 6% to 8%." In regard to the general population, the only significant study was one from a family practice clinic. They asked 350 consecutive patients to fill out anonymous questionnaires in which they were asked questions like "Have you ever done anything to deliberately prolong an illness?" Seven percent said they had, including things like exposing themselves to substances they were allergic to.

A modern twist on the disorder has been dubbed *Munchausen by Internet*. This describes the person who goes online to different health forums and fakes their illness. In extreme cases, they may post their own web pages describing their illness, treatment, and progress in great detail. Again, these frauds may be seeking not only attention but money as well. They may offer a link that allows web page visitors to donate. Although some may genuinely have Munchausen syndrome, many are simply scam artists.

Scientific Take: A Cry for Attention

While Munchausen syndrome is certainly a psychological problem, the underlying cause is not fully understood. Researchers have pinpointed a few possible explanations. Deeply distressing or disturbing experiences as a child may lead to the behavior. Mental imbalance or a personality disorder could contribute.

The National Health Service in England adds that a deep-rooted grudge against health care professionals or authority figures may provoke an individual to develop Munchausen syndrome. Childhood trauma, parental neglect, or abandonment may lead to the condition, which spurs patients to seek constant attention. They have an unnatural need to be the center of attention, a desire to be cared for by others, or both. One theory holds that the afflicted are punishing themselves by making themselves feel sick or injured.

The National Health Service lists these personality disorders that are thought to be connected with Munchausen syndrome:

- Antisocial personality disorder—a person may take pleasure in **manipulating** and deceiving doctors, giving them a sense of power and control.
- Borderline personality disorder—where a person struggles to control their feelings and often swings between positive and negative views of others.
- **Narcissistic** personality disorder—where a person often swings between seeing themselves as special and fearing they're worthless.

Symptoms to look out for are

- Pretending to have psychological symptoms—for example, claiming to hear voices or claiming to see things that aren't really there.

- Pretending to have physical symptoms—for example, claiming to have chest pain or a stomachache.
- Actively trying to get ill—such as deliberately infecting a wound by rubbing dirt into it.

People with Munchausen's can be very manipulative and are sometimes willing to inflict serious injury upon themselves to make themselves ill or wounded.

To treat the syndrome, medical professionals use a combination of psychoanalysis and cognitive behavioral therapy (CBT). CBT is a method to help a patient recognize unhelpful and unrealistic beliefs and replace them with more rational ones. Psychoanalysis helps uncover unconscious motivations or buried traumas that may be tied to the behavior.

Although it is not known how common the condition is, it is considered rare. Studies have revealed that the disorder occurs most often among 20- to 40-year-old women, who often have a background in health care, and unmarried white men, between the ages of 30 and 50.

Munchausen by Proxy Syndrome (MBPS)

In this related form of Munchausen's (which is sometimes called *factitious* disorder by proxy), a caregiver induces or fakes illness in the person under their care. Most cases involve a mother and child. The mother may add blood to a child's urine or stool or heat a thermometer to indicate a false fever. Some may go as far as to cause symptoms through poisoning, provoking an infection, or suffocation.

The individual exhibiting this criminal behavior is often a medical professional of some type. They know how to cause illness or impairment without killing the patient, and medical professionals can often be reluctant to doubt them, thinking that a concerned, loving caretaker would not inflict such harm.

In 2014, Julie Gregory revealed her childhood battle with a mother who had MBPS in her autobiography, *Sickened: Memoir of a Lost Childhood*. As a child, her mother would take her from doctor to doctor insisting that she had a heart defect that none of them could seem to detect.

Even though Julie felt fine most of her young life, her mother would often tell her that she had to stay home from school because she was sick. Sometimes, her mother gave her a pill that would cause her to have a horrible headache.

An interview with Munchausen by proxy victim author Julie Gregory.

On the way to the hospital once, her mother bashed her head against a car window to make sure she had a physical problem. She would also starve her daughter so she became underweight and lightheaded. Once at a hospital, Julie would eat ravenously. When she was 13, she hit a point where she had to fight back against her mother. During one of her many visits to the hospital, a nurse told her that they were going to cut her open and put a catheter directly into her heart. That's when she bolted upright in her bed and said, "My mom is making this up!!" Her plea helped her escape the endless cycle of abuse from her mother.

Looking back, Julie thinks her mother's behavior may have been triggered by a very troubled childhood, that may have included rape. Her mother's abuse toward her has led to a challenging adulthood for Julie. She has avoided doctors, not trusting that they know what they're doing. She carries emotional scars, longing for the normal childhood of which her mother robbed her.

Scientific Take: An Angel in Disguise

As with Munchausen syndrome, adults with MBPS have a psychological disorder that drives them to want attention and appear as self-sacrificing and devoted. Investigators have found that many with MBPS had been abused physically, emotionally, or sexually as children. The child of a parent with MBPS needs to get protection and the parent needs psychotherapy and perhaps medication.

Medical experts have debated whether those with MBPS are criminals, sick, or a combination of both. Dr. Marc Feldman of the University of Alabama has studied the disorder for years. He says that about 600 to 1,200 cases are reported in the United States annually.

Children are most often the victims in cases of Munchausen by proxy syndrome.

Those looking to prevent such abuse should look for these symptoms among caregivers:

- They describe a child's medical issues in great detail.
- They tend to be extremely involved in the child's health care and often refuse to leave the child's bedside.
- They are seen as overly devoted.
- They may lie a lot.

Children who have such a caretaker may be in and out of the hospital an unusual number of times, and they have strange or extreme symptoms of illness.

Other Stories of MBPS

Lacey Spears was known as a mommy blogger—she chronicled her young son's health problems on Facebook, Twitter, and a personal blog titled "Garnett's Journey." From a very early age,

Garnett was frequently taken to the emergency room with vomiting, seizures, bleeding ear infections, and digestive problems. He was hospitalized 23 times in his short life. When Lacey was living in Florida, neighbors called state authorities worried about the child's health. In 2012 when she moved to a commune in New York, the community showered her in attention and praise for being such a dutiful mother to her sick son. At age 5, Garnett died after Lacey force fed him high doses of sodium followed by drinks of water that made his brain swell. The 27-year-old mother was sentenced to 20 years to life in prison for murdering her son.

Eight-year-old Jennifer Bush had been hospitalized more than 200 times, and she had received more than 40 medical procedures. Doctors had removed her gall bladder, appendix, and some of her small intestine. Her health would improve with each hospital visit and deteriorate rapidly with each return to her mother. Nurses became suspicious and one spied the mother injecting something into Jennifer's mouth. After her mother was arrested, Kathy's eating returned to normal. In 1999, her mother was convicted of aggravated child abuse.

Angels of Mercy

Throughout history, there have been several health care providers who intentionally killed their patients. Called angels of mercy or angels of death, many have gained the reputation of being prolific serial killers. In the United Kingdom, Beverly Allitt was given 13 life sentences in 1993 for murdering four children, attempting to murder another three, and causing grievous bodily harm to six more at a hospital in Lincolnshire, England. The nurse carried out the crimes between 1991 and 1993, and was diagnosed as suffering from Munchausen syndrome by proxy. New Jersey nurse Charles Cullen was given six life sentences in 2006 for the murder of 40 patients (though he was suspected of causing up to 400 deaths) over a 16-year stretch. He said that he gave victims lethal injections to end their suffering.

Series Glossary

Affliction: Something that causes pain or suffering.

Afterlife: Life after death.

Anthropologist: A professional who studies the origin, development, and behavioral aspects of human beings and their societies, especially primitive societies.

Apparition: A ghost or ghostlike image of a person.

Archaeologist: A person who studies human history and prehistory through the excavation of sites and the analysis of artifacts and other physical remains found.

Automaton: A person who acts in a mechanical, machinelike way as if in trance.

Bipolar disorder: A mental condition marked by alternating periods of elation and depression.

Catatonic: To be in a daze or stupor.

Celestial: Relating to the sky or heavens.

Charlatan: A fraud.

Chronic: Continuing for a long time; used to describe an illness or medical condition generally lasting longer than three months.

Clairvoyant: A person who claims to have a supernatural ability to perceive events in the future or beyond normal sensory contact.

Cognition: The mental action or process of acquiring knowledge and understanding through thought, experience, and the senses.

Déjà vu: A sensation of experiencing something that has happened before when experienced for the first time.

Delirium: A disturbed state of mind characterized by confusion, disordered speech, and hallucinations.

Dementia: A chronic mental condition caused by brain disease or injury and characterized by memory disorders, personality changes, and impaired reasoning.

Dissociative: Related to a breakdown of mental function that normally operates smoothly, such as memory and consciousness. Dissociative identity disorder is a mental Trauma: A deeply distressing or disturbing experience.

Divine: Relating to God or a god.

Ecstatic: A person subject to mystical experiences.

Elation: Great happiness.

Electroencephalogram (EEG): A test that measures and records the electrical activity of the brain.

Endorphins: Hormones secreted within the brain and nervous system that trigger a positive feeling in the body.

ESP (extrasensory perception): An ability to communicate or understand outside of normal sensory capability, such as in telepathy and clairvoyance.

Euphoria: An intense state of happiness; elation.

Hallucinate: To experience a perception of something that seems real but is not actually present.

Immortal: Living forever.

Inhibition: A feeling that makes one self-conscious and unable to act in a relaxed and natural way.

Involuntary: Not subject to a person's control.

Karma: A Buddhist belief that whatever one does comes back—a person's actions can determine his or her reincarnation.

Levitate: To rise in the air by supernatural or magical power.

Malevolent: Evil.

Malignant: Likely to grow and spread in a fast and uncontrolled way that can cause death.

Mayhem: Chaos.

Mesmerize: To hold someone's attention so that he or she notices nothing else.

Mindfulness: A meditation practice for bringing one's attention to the internal and external experiences occurring in the present moment.

Monolith: A giant, single upright block of stone, especially as a monument.

Motivational: Designed to promote a willingness to do or achieve something.

Motor functions: Muscle and nerve acts that produce motion. Fine motor functions include writing and tying shoes; gross motor functions are large movements such as walking and kicking.

Mystics: People who have supernatural knowledge or experiences; they have a supposed insight into spirituality and mysteries transcending ordinary human knowledge.

Necromancy: An ability to summon and control things that are dead.

Neurological: Related to the nervous system or neurology (a branch of medicine concerning diseases and disorders of the nervous system).

Neuroplasticity: The ability of the brain to form and reorganize synaptic connections, especially in response to learning or experience, or following injury.

Neuroscientist: One who studies the nervous system

Neurotransmitters: Chemicals released by nerve fibers that transmit signals across a synapse (the gap between nerve cells).

Occult: Of or relating to secret knowledge of supernatural things.

Olfactory: Relating to the sense of smell.

Out-of-body experience: A sensation of being outside one's body, floating above and observing events, often when unconscious or clinically dead.

Papyrus: A material prepared in ancient Egypt from the pithy stem of a water plant, used to make sheets for writing or painting on, rope, sandals, and boats.

Paralysis: An inability to move or act.

Paranoid: Related to a mental condition involving intense anxious or fearful feelings and thoughts often related to persecution, threat, or conspiracy.

Paranormal: Beyond the realm of the normal; outside of commonplace scientific understanding.

Paraphysical: Not part of the physical word; often used in relation to supernatural occurrences.

Parapsychologist: A person who studies paranormal and psychic phenomena.

Parapsychology: Study of paranormal and psychic phenomena considered inexplicable in the world of traditional psychology.

Phobia: Extreme irrational fear.

Physiologist: A person who studies the workings of living systems.

Precognition: Foreknowledge of an event through some sort of ESP.

Premonition: A strong feeling that something is about to happen, especially something unpleasant.

Pseudoscience: Beliefs or practices that may appear scientific, but have not been proven by any scientific method.

Psychiatric: Related to mental illness or its treatment.

Psychic: Of or relating to the mind; often used to describe mental powers that science cannot explain.

Psychokinesis: The ability to move or manipulate objects using the mind alone.

Psychological: Related to the mental and emotional state of a person.

PTSD: Post-traumatic stress disorder is a mental health condition triggered by a terrifying event.

Repository: A place, receptacle, or structure where things are stored.

Resilient: Able to withstand or recover quickly from difficult conditions.

Resonate: To affect or appeal to someone in a personal or emotional way.

Schizophrenia: A severe mental disorder characterized by an abnormal grasp of reality; symptoms can include hallucinations and delusions.

Skeptic: A person who questions or doubts particular things.

Spectral: Ghostly.

Spiritualism: A religious movement that believes the spirits of the dead can communicate with the living.

Stimulus: Something that causes a reaction.

Subconscious: The part of the mind that we are not aware of but that influences our thoughts, feelings, and behaviors.

Sumerians: An ancient civilization/people (5400–1750 BCE) in the region known as Mesopotamia (modern day Iraq and Kuwait).

Synapse: A junction between two nerve cells.

Synthesize: To combine a number of things into a coherent whole.

Telekinesis: Another term for psychokinesis. The ability to move or manipulate objects using the mind alone.

Telepathy: Communication between people using the mind alone and none of the five senses.

Uncanny: Strange or mysterious.

Further Resources

Websites

National Alliance on Mental Illness: *www.nami.org/*
The nation's largest grassroots mental health organization dedicated to building better lives for the millions of Americans affected by mental illness.

International Society for the Study of Trauma and Dissociation: *www.isst-d.org/default.asp?contentID=9*
An organization dedicated to teaching about complex trauma and dissociation.

Foreign Accent Syndrome—University of Texas at Dallas: *www.utdallas.edu/research/FAS/*
A website designed to provide support to those seeking information about this rare speech disorder.

Lewy Body Dementia Association, Capgras Syndrome in DLB Associated with Anxiety and Hallucinations: *www.lbda.org/content/capgras-syndrome-dlb-associated-anxiety-and-hallucinations-0*
Information on Capgras syndrome as it relates to dementia.

Child Welfare Information Gateway, Perpetrators of Munchausen Syndrome by Proxy: *www.childwelfare.gov/topics/can/perpetrators/perp-munchausen/*
How to identify perpetrators and take action.

Movies

Here are a few movies related to some of the strange mental disorders in this book:

***Split* (2017)**
M. Night Shyamalan's thriller about a kidnapper diagnosed with 23 distinct personalities.

***Invasion of the Body Snatchers* (1956)**
A science fiction movie about a small-town doctor who learns that the population of his community is being replaced by emotionless alien duplicates. Note that people with Capgras syndrome believe this phenomena can be true.

***The Good Mother* (2013)**
The good mother is, in fact, a bad mother with Munchausen by proxy syndrome. After her best friend dies, a teen discovers that the girl's mother deliberately made her sick.

Further Reading

Baring-Gold, S. *The Book of Werewolves: The Classic Study of Lycanthropy.* Page Turner, 2004.

Bellows, Alan. *Alien Hand Syndrome and Other Too-Weird-Not-To-Be-True Stories.* New York: Workman Publishing, 2009.

DiClaudio, Dennis. *The Paranoid's Pocket Guide to Mental Disorders You Can Just Feel Coming On.* London: Bloomsbury, 2007.

Gregory, Julie. *Sickened: The True Story of a Lost Childhood.* New York: Bantam, 2004.

Haddock, Deborah. *The Dissociative Identity Disorder Sourcebook.* New York: McGraw-Hill Education, 2001.

Kreisman, Jerold. *Sometimes I Act Crazy: Living with Borderline Personality Disorder.* Hoboken, NJ: Wiley, 2006.

Powers, Richard. *The Echo Maker.* New York: Picador, 2007 (novel involving Capgras syndrome).

Ramachandran, V.S. and Sandra Blakeslee. *Phantoms in the Brain: Probing the Mysteries of the Human Mind.* New York: William Morrow, 1999.

Sacks, Oliver. *The Man Who Mistook His Wife for a Hat.* New York: Touchstone, 1998.

About the Author

Don Rauf has written more than 30 nonfiction books, including *Killer Lipstick and Other Spy Gadgets, Simple Rules for Card Games, Psychology of Serial Killers: Historical Serial Killers, The French and Indian War, The Rise and Fall of the Ottoman Empire,* and *George Washington's Farewell Address.* He has contributed to the books *Weird Canada* and *American Inventions.* He lives in Seattle with his wife, Monique, and son, Leo.

Index